SISTAS STAY STRONG

A BOOK OF POEMS FOR QUEENS

ERIC REESE

Copyright © 2018 by Eric Reese

All rights reserved.

No part of this book may be reproduced in any form or by any electronic or mechanical means, including information storage and retrieval systems, without written permission from the author, except for the use of brief quotations in a book review.

ISBN: 978-1-925988-36-9

NOTABLE MENTIONS

Dear Eric, thanks for writing. Receiving emails from everyday Americans across our country was one of the best parts of my job as President, and I continue to be touched by stories like yours.

In the extraordinary diversity of opinions and experiences that make up our national character, we see the common sense of purpose and inherent goodness that have always defined who we are as Americans. I appreciate your writing, and I wish you and your loved ones the very best.

— Sincerely, Barack Obama

MY SISTA'

For every sista' out there trying to live her best life!

CONTENTS

Guilty	1
Gangstas Paradise	2
Do me	3
Give Thanks	4
Revenge is a Bitch	5
Jobless	6
Harsh Reality	7
Isn't that so?	8
Couldn't imagine	9
Hey Betty!	10
Generation Next	11
Fairytales	12
Yeah Right	13
These days	14
Rosa Parks lives on	15
Black Widow	16
Who's the Master	17
Someone knew	18
When is this over?	19
Mother's Love	20
They watchin'	21
Can I live?	22
Be you, not me	23
Daddy gone mad!	24
American Idol	25
Where's my justice?	26
My Brother	27
Mother's Keeper	28
Feel me?	29

That's Deep	30
He's a racist	31
Relief is coming	32
Now you understand	33
Which gun was that?	34
Fucked up	35
Don't Hate on Us	36
Ya Mama!	37
My Babies and their Gangstas	38
Lips	39
IDGAF	40
Somebody	41
Deeper	42
Let me grieve	43
Long ride ahead	44
My Money, Your Lost	45
She's going to be great one day!	46
Really tho?	47
2016	48
Am I kidding?	49
What if…2020	50
You go Sista'	51
Of course!	52
Nursing Episode	53
Damn!	54
Pay me!	55
That's Me	56
Momma knows best	57
It wasn't because of the sex	58
Survival of the Fittest	59
Sista go get it	60
You be the judge	61
Take note	62
I'm done	63

Mercy	64
Savage	65
Ya Point?	66
Skinwashed	67
Damn shame	68
You already know…	69
Sellin' ya soul	70
BWWM 1935	71
I know that's right	72
Lies, Lies, Lies	73
Thank You	74
#metoo in 1985	75
Media playin' games	76
She's my sister not sista'	77
BW Bequest	78
Ready to confess?	79
Sista' live on	80
About Eric Reese	81

GUILTY

They raped me,
but the judge said
that the guilty one
was me
for being black
and a woman.

GANGSTAS PARADISE

The worst thing
about being a gang member's wife
is not knowing
if he would be alive come dinner time.

DO ME

She never cried
because her spouse left her,
didn't have time for it;
when you have five mouths to feed,
the tears are secondary.

GIVE THANKS

"She
had been
the best mother
of all,
despite
being
the only servant
of our family."

REVENGE IS A BITCH

One day, white men would pay
for what they did to her;
couldn't just come
to humiliate her
and kill her son
without consequences.

JOBLESS

They didn't
give me the job;
apparently one of
the requirements
for the position
was not to be black.

HARSH REALITY

I wanted to go
to the same places as them,
get in their fine baths,
but for being of color
I just ended
with my reflection
in the turbid water
of the basin.

ISN'T THAT SO?

He was cheating
on his wife
with the woman
of color
in the corner,

and then
he
repudiated
her
in public,

the perfect alibi.

COULDN'T IMAGINE

It was difficult being black,
but being the only one
in a white village
in 1920
was just
hell.

HEY BETTY!

His mother attacked me;
apparently, she couldn't accept that
her son would have a daughter
with a black woman.

GENERATION NEXT

"Daughter,
you are beautiful
and *no one*
can tell you otherwise"
said my mother

while my grandmother
shouted at me
for having braids.

FAIRYTALES

Could have
the stature,
the elegance
and the poise,
but as I was not
a blue-eyed blonde,
I should forget
all my years practicing
runway walk
in my little room.

YEAH RIGHT

The police took her money;
she was told that
blacks would not have "much"
without having gone through
other people's bags.

THESE DAYS

They called her
crazy
only by repeating
the white speech
about respect
being blind to color.

ROSA PARKS LIVES ON

She didn't want to
give her spot
to the white man,

she was arrested;

he laughed,
but she began
a rebellion years later.

BLACK WIDOW

Children were starving
to death
and no one did anything
to help her.

Which of her crimes
was worse,
being black
or the spouse
of an ex-convict?

WHO'S THE MASTER

She was afraid of his master,
knew that whenever
he visited her at night,
her crotch would end up wounded.

SOMEONE KNEW

They took her son
for being half-blooded;
they didn't want
the public to know
he was the son of the cook.

WHEN IS THIS OVER?

She wanted
to shine,
sing
and be known
all over the world.

Instead,
she was forced
to wash up, shut up
and prayed that
her mistress was
in a good mood
that day.

MOTHER'S LOVE

I preferred to kill my children
with my own hands
rather than give them
to those armored white men.

THEY WATCHIN'

Luckily, he fell in love
with her skin color;
unluckily, that was
the same reason
that led to his death.

CAN I LIVE?

She was looking
at the television and dreaming
of being one of those actresses;

next second, her husband was shouting
at her and she returned to a reality
where she was looked down on.

BE YOU, NOT ME

She wanted to
be rich and white,
so her stepfather
couldn't
abuse her
and her mother
wouldn't
throw dirt on her face.

DADDY GONE MAD!

Her daughter asked
what had happened to her eye
and she told her
that she had fallen;

she said that
hidden in the bathroom,
while her husband
was looking for his shotgun.

AMERICAN IDOL

"In America
you can be

who you want,

but it's true
only

if you're male
and white."

WHERE'S MY JUSTICE?

Wouldn't let her have an abortion,
insisting it was more moral

to force her
to give birth
to the son

of the man
who raped her on her birthday.

MY BROTHER

The slave was freed
and wept,
not for joy
but for having lost most
of his life
cleaning up
after white women's asses.

MOTHER'S KEEPER

She was killed only
for not letting them beat her;
the world won a heroine,
I lost my mother.

FEEL ME?

Took the child
from the pile of corpses
and little she cared
over being called crazy
for taking a white boy home.
For her, the right to life was blind.

THAT'S DEEP

"When I leave home,
the first thing I do
is ask God to take care of me
and get me away from
some bad white character."
Said a girl
before even knowing
the meaning of these words.

HE'S A RACIST

Feared that father
would find and kill her.
At that time, the color of skin
was more important
than love.

RELIEF IS COMING

The woman strained
by feeling the hug of the white girl,
after years of receiving abuse from her family,
she was surprised to find some affection.

NOW YOU UNDERSTAND

From my black neighbor I learned that tears,
regardless of the weeper, are all of the same color.
At the end, all is the same: sadness.

WHICH GUN WAS THAT?

She took the phone
and pretended to laugh
rather than be crying,
"I may not come home tonight"
the man stood silently
with the gun to her head.

FUCKED UP

She couldn't leave him,
because he would somehow know
she was cheating on him
with a white man.

DON'T HATE ON US

She boasted that
her son graduated with honors
from the best university in town.
Some looked on with hate,
but that was something
the family was already used to.

YA MAMA!

She died giving birth.
The doctor said that
they didn't accept
"black rats".

MY BABIES AND THEIR GANGSTAS

All of her daughters
were married and went to live
with gang members,
sometimes she repented
of having not moved
from the neighborhood
when she had the opportunity.

LIPS

She was the envy of all
with her huge red lips.
More than makeup,
her best kept secret:
arguing
with her boyfriend.

IDGAF

Spat at her boss
in the face.
Got arrested.
So?
Working there
was worse
than going to prison.

SOMEBODY

I never understood
how with that attitude,
she was able to be considered
the best member of her family.
Perhaps because
she always reminded
the nagging aunt.

DEEPER

She looked at her man
and sighed with regret,
if she had known
that the chocolate bar
would become a small square,
then she wouldn't have removed it
from the wrapping.

LET ME GRIEVE

She cried bitterly
when her deceased
spouse's brothers
moved her
from their home;
they wouldn't allow
the "slag" to live there.

LONG RIDE AHEAD

I may be 80 years old,
but the creature
she has in her belly
has much life to live yet.
My gift for them
is a nice train trip.

MY MONEY, YOUR LOST

She finally could buy that outfit,
but something
went terribly wrong:
The seller didn't like the idea
of having a
black customer in the store.

SHE'S GOING TO BE GREAT ONE DAY!

Rose her hand
hoping to be the one
who could solve the problem
on the green board,
but the Professor ignored her
and preferred a white boy
to give the wrong answer.

REALLY THO?

Despite seeing him
as a lonely creature,
they wouldn't adopt him
because her husband said
'I don't like the color'.

2016

If a white woman's
vote was wrong,
a black one
doing the same
was just insane.

AM I KIDDING?

Darling, don't cry
because this young man left you,
I've been black my whole life,
everyone have rejected me
at some point
and see the smile
that I have yet to give you."

WHAT IF...2020

She can provide
a good future for our country,
but she's an African American,
so is it better to vote
for the Tycoon
who will take us to our ruin?

YOU GO SISTA'

For the Lord's sake,
I studied the law
to defend the rights
of African-American women,
not their rapists!

OF COURSE!

Was accused of murder
when she was just
avoiding her rape.

NURSING EPISODE

Five years in university
to just finish
cleaning
an old woman's
underwear.

DAMN!

They took away
her son and husband,
and still asked the reason
why her family was hated
so much by those
who were not of same color.

PAY ME!

She was tired
of singing and receiving
meager tips
while her blonde friend
got everything.

THAT'S ME

Got tired of work
on the cotton plantation,
only to find dirty dishes to clean
and diapers to change.
She wondered
"who the hell
is the owner
of this house then?"

MOMMA KNOWS BEST

She was trying
to make up the bruise,
her husband gave her;
she didn't want her mother
to say "I told you so".

IT WASN'T BECAUSE OF THE SEX

Women slaves
found themselves afraid
while the cry of the victim that night
came out of the study
with their master.

SURVIVAL OF THE FITTEST

They forced her to see
her husband hung
and son raped;
even so, she kept saving
so much hatred,
that she learned to forgive
the hour that she passed away.

SISTA GO GET IT

She didn't know anything
other than being in the kitchen
but wasn't intimidated
when she discovered that
she had the same power
to generate money in it
like her white counterparts.

YOU BE THE JUDGE

If she sues, they would kill her,
if she stayed at home, they would do the same thing;
so, she took his gun
and decided to put an end to his life.
At least, she decided when and how to die.

TAKE NOTE

When a charismatic
controversial
scientist was asked
from where his intelligence
and success came,
he said: "I was breastfed
by a black woman;
that was the secret: Love."

I'M DONE

Her son was ill,
but the doctors weren't allowed
to help slaves.

MERCY

She cried
while healing
her brother's wounds,
that day they exceeded
in punishments.

SAVAGE

Only said to the lady of the house
that the dress didn't look nice on her,
it wasn't necessary to respond
by hitting her across the head with a vase.

YA POINT?

Surgeries
can't solve life problems;
I did it to my buttocks
and they still call me
"black ass".

SKINWASHED

So many creams
to lighten my skin
just left me
cancer
and problems
with my people.

DAMN SHAME

Had to say
'goodbye'
to my beautiful
Afro
only to let me
keep the job.

YOU ALREADY KNOW...

"I work more
than them
and yet
I earn less,

guess why?"

SELLIN' YA SOUL

I was tired
of walking down the street
and ashamed for my color,
one day we had to finish this,
but meanwhile,
I'm looking for something
that can cover my expenses.

BWWM 1935

He wanted to take care of me
and they killed him
for having spoken with a black woman.

I KNOW THAT'S RIGHT

Singing
was the only way
for us to feel
some sort of
freedom
in the evenings.

LIES, LIES, LIES

He said that
the reason why
he raped me
was because
God has to punish
people like me.

THANK YOU

I just wanted to be happy
and God made me
a woman of color
in doing so.

#METOO IN 1985

I should defend
my rights as a woman,
I couldn't sit and wait
while they abused my sisters
and nobody was doing anything.

MEDIA PLAYIN' GAMES

A white boy
brings a weapon
from his father to school
and somehow,
they blame mental illness
just because of color,
despite not being present
at the time of the incident.

SHE'S MY SISTER NOT SISTA'

"They say that
black women are a waste,
but I wish I could be a waste too,
so I can sing like that."

BW BEQUEST

Her last words were:
"Take care
of these children
as I did;
I couldn't bear
that you might
take away
so much love
I've given to them."

READY TO CONFESS?

"I didn't care
to take a slap in the face
from my former slave girl.
She had finally won the war
and I fairly deserved far more
because of what
I've done to her sisters."

SISTA' LIVE ON

"I took a trip
to a community in the U.S.A.
This society was invested entirely
by people of color.
It was the closest thing to a utopia.
When I asked their leader
(a woman, surprisingly)
how they created this,
she said that instead of
wasting time and energy
on the past and hatred,
they used it for more
food, health and education."

ABOUT ERIC REESE

Eric Reese was born and raised in Philadelphia, Pennsylvania and was the recipient of the first Mayoral Scholarship of Philadelphia (1993) and the Philadelphia Federation of Teachers Human Relations Award (1989).

You can reach Eric at feekness@gmail.com.

www.ingramcontent.com/pod-product-compliance
Lightning Source LLC
Chambersburg PA
CBHW021120080526
44587CB00010B/582